Yellow Plum Season

Yellow Plum Season
黃梅季節

Pui Ying Wong

The New York Quarterly Foundation, Inc.
New York, New York

NYQ Books™ is an imprint of The New York Quarterly Foundation, Inc.

The New York Quarterly Foundation, Inc.
P. O. Box 2015
Old Chelsea Station
New York, NY 10113

www.nyqbooks.org

Copyright © 2010 by Pui Ying Wong

All rights reserved. No part of this book may be used or reproduced in any manner whatsoever without written permission of the author. This book is a work of fiction. Any references to historical events, real people or real locales are used fictitiously. Other names, characters, places, and incidents are products of the author's imagination, and any resemblance to actual events or locales or persons, living or dead, is entirely coincidental.

First Edition

Set in New Baskerville

Interior Layout and Design by Raymond P. Hammond
Cover Layout and Design by Tara Sinn | www.terrrrific.com

Library of Congress Control Number: 2010907952

ISBN: 978-1-935520-29-0

For Tim

&

Damon, in memory

Acknowledgments

Some of these poems appeared in the following journals: *The Asian Pacific American Journal, Blue Fifth Review, Cavalier Literary Couture, Chiron Review, DMQ Review, 5 AM, The New York Quarterly,* and *Poetz*; and in these two chapbooks: *Mementos*, Finishing Line Press, 2007, and *Sonnet for a New Country*, Pudding House Press, 2008.

Contents

I.

The Fir Tree in the Marina / 17
Montorgueil / 18
Pére Lachaise / 20
After "Landscape near Auvers" by Van Gogh / 21
High Stake Travel / 22
China after Mao / 23
Village in the North / 24
The Underpass at O'Hare Airport / 25
Visiting My Sister in Australia / 26
Trouville / 27
Yellow Plum Season / 28

II.

New Heart / 35
Dipping into the Black Pool… / 36
First Moving Day / 37
Egg Woman / 38
Monsoon (1967) / 39
Yesterday Morning / 40
Even in Dreams There Are Reasons / 41
Self-Portrait as a Fluorescent Lamp / 42
While a Fever Burns Time Is Elongated / 44
How to Live in a Funk / 45

Mementos / 46
Asleep in a Foreign City after a Long Flight / 47
A Hat for the Sea, Two Voices / 48
If / 50
Tsunami / 51
Afterward / 52
The Elm Tree in front of the Pharmacy / 53
Sonnet for an Ant / 54
Repair / 55
Sonnet for a New Country / 56
My Poet / 57
Looking out to Java Road on a Cloudless Day / 58
The Blue Jays / 60

III.

Vantage Point / 65
If the Angels Are Watching / 66
Beslan / 67
Strawberries / 68
The Believer / 69
Difficult Music / 70
At Diner Retro / 72
A Rap for Prophet Isaiah / 73
Between the Raids / 74
A Woman in Brooklyn Says… / 75
Under the Expressway / 76
Sweet and Bitter / 77
Turtle Soup Song / 78

Hudson in July   / 79
Fate   / 80
The Reader Speaks to the Poet   / 81
In Praise of a Rainy Day   / 82
At Crate & Barrel   / 83
May and Lilacs   / 84
Letter to K   / 85
Inexhaustible Days   / 86
The Moon from My Writing Table   / 88
Notes from My Flight Book   / 89

*Time takes life away
and gives us memory, gold with flame,
black with embers.*

Adam Zagajewski

I.

船塢旁的冷杉樹
(The Fir Tree in the Marina)

沿着海灣
設了一個臨時的遊藝團
那裏有七彩的旗幟
碰碰車和小丑
但沒有多少遊客
只有少許工人
携着藍色的漁具箱
微風吹了一整天
時帶陣陣毛雨
我們不過在昨天才到
但好像坐了坐不完的車程
很多小鎮變得朦朧
我們嘗試用陌生的語言
和總是指向他處的路標
來確定所在的地方
在之前的一個車站
我們看見山上的白教堂
有些乘客下車
一個是盲的　另一個用輪椅
其他便恐怕
有埋在深處的傷痕
我擔心會忘記
那帶着奇蹟的月台
我們是否要走這麼遠
才能找到
那還容我們活下去的國度？
在船塢的盡頭
有棵冷杉垂懸在長櫈上
一對穿上雨披的男女
正從饑餓的霧中走出

THE FIR TREE IN THE MARINA

Along the basin
A carnival has set up
There are color banners
Bumper cars and a clown
But there's hardly anyone
Just a few workers
Carrying blue tackle boxes
All day there's a breeze
A drizzle here and there
We have arrived only yesterday
After what seems days on the train
Many towns of course were a blur
We tried to learn where we were
With languages we didn't know
And signs that always point elsewhere
At the stop before this we saw
A white church sitting on a hill
Then some passengers got off
One blind and another in a wheelchair
The rest must have wounds
Wedging somewhere deep
I was afraid that I might forget
This platform of miracles
Do we have to travel this far
To find what world is still possible?
At the end of the dock
A fir tree drapes over the bench
A man and a woman in ponchos
Walking out of the hungry fog

MONTORGUEIL

1. The Laundromat

It rains on end. Mad heart.
A single washer buzzes
like a trapped bee,
in the last spin cycle.

2. Marché U

The gypsy woman waits.
Her bucket of ruined peonies
have soaked up enough rain
to douse out a fire
of birds frenzy in heat.

3. The bakery

There is white dough on the white table.
There is white flour on the white floor.
There is the baker, turning up his face
to a world raining white.

4. The sex shop

The bouncer is smoking in front
of the rain slick mural, a cartoon of women
with enormous breasts and snake thin waists.

The hostess steps out. She wears a big blond wig,
looking bored. Quietly he lights her cigarette,
there they stand side by side watching the rain pass.

5. The studio on Rue Saint Sauveur

The window opens to other windows.
The sky is a gondola of time forgotten.
At night we write on a wooden desk.
Outside there's no cry for blood
and the guillotine,
just light dying on the cobbled street.

PÉRE LACHAISE

Uphill, then downhill
deep in the cemetery
greenway crammed with graves

But we have maps, sold
in every flower shop, all
on Rue Gambetta

We veer tomb to tomb
reading names off grime-flecked stones
in plane tree shadow

Statues of weeping
Magdalene, angels with wings
too heavy to fly

Behind the temple
Jim Morrison's "a white ball
of fire," wrote a fan

Hear the music, hard
as it punctures and punctures
we keep migrating

Remember hunger
that burns like insomnia
may have led us here?

AFTER "LANDSCAPE NEAR AUVERS" BY VAN GOGH

Why not? Let calm descend like a fine mist,
let clouds whirl and run on the canvas, but
not despairing. We need a day like this,
a day we can see far. Take in the wheatfields,
vast as the lover's heart in which you roam
naked. Take in the small sea of cornflowers,
heaving poppies and believe in their beauty.
Let the wolf prey upon the animals
for they are safe under their keeper's watch.
Let nothing break the calm. See mounds of hay
fuzz to gold in the sun and the olive trees
wind around low hills into the ether.
See beyond this room bleached in miseries
big and small threatening to pull us in.

HIGH STAKE TRAVEL

I found the self-check counter
in the terminal. I touched
the screen, a voice came on,
swift and meticulous
to command me: *insert
your card in the card slot.*
What card? I was stumped.
any card? Panic in the omnipresent
digital gods.
                The he-voice refrained:
insert your card in the card slot.
I fumbled, dumped out my wallet
on the Formica counter:
credit card, mileage card, debit card,
library card, discount cards
to Pathmark, Rite-Aid Pharmacy,
Popular Books (a bookstore chain
in Hong Kong, my birth city), an expired
calling card, New York State driver's license,
Hong Kong resident identity card, Chinese
non-resident permit card (to enter
the mother country).

I mapped them out, by function,
by year, by country, each one makes the other,
and told him: *pick.*

CHINA AFTER MAO

(YangShuo, 2000)

Red still dazzles. Not
the hot, wavy summer:
Tinnanmen Square, 1966
where a generation
thrust into the torrid air
his *little red book*—

but in a newly sequined
bridal gown, worn now
by a faceless mannequin—

A young village woman
gazes at it, and imagines

the red sash falling off
her shoulders
when the mandarin collar
becomes unfastened
by a hand
not yet known.

VILLAGE IN THE NORTH

At dusk the villagers come to greet us,
visitors who've arrived in SUVs.
One by one they fill the square shrouded in dust,
the retired teachers, the town clerks, the thieves.
Our group leader, a bespectacled man,
starts to speak about what these people lack:
water, electricity that they can
count on, soil that can grow food. The air smacks
of goat shit fermenting in the background.
He says children need their books and vaccines,
the old their pensions. Many seem spellbound,
some fidget. The sky lights a reddish sheen
over the plain, turning us all a shad-glow
that we can neither wipe off nor bestow.

THE UNDERPASS AT O'HARE AIRPORT

We move between the terminals lugging
baby strollers, laptops and backpacks. Like

sedated warriors we travel in parallel
to points of joy or heartbreak.

In the chamber, the walls are warped
to imitate waves. Behind the opaque glass panels,

pink corals glow. For a moment,
it's as if we were underwater

like they would have us believe, that we're inside
some primordial womb of a whale.

And if God is on our side, we'll be spewed out
like Jonah in three days—the world made new,

love returns. We move along weightless,
speechless on the conveyor belt, staring

straight ahead, listen to words of caution
issued from the P.A.—omnipresent,

urgent, repeating itself, oblivious to where
we have been, and to where we will go.

VISITING MY SISTER IN AUSTRALIA

Smog in the sky, bushfire burning outside
the city. The constellation has changed.
I'm under. The years peel off like old skin.
My sister sipping coffee, her eyes wide;
between us, a blooming walnut tree. Strange
all these fruits, maybe spring won't go to ruin
after all. December, this side of world,
sprigs of green fruits round into each other.
It took us forever to count, moments
long enough to freeze a heartache— unfurl
and release. If memories can sever
from their roots, will they become sacrament
too like harvest fruits we put in a dish?
Cut one open, the meat is babyish.

TROUVILLE

For Tim

The slot machine turns, for half a Euro,
three laughing Buddha rise to the payline
and the coins drop to the tray like water.
I know this casino can be anywhere
with lights blinking mad gold and crimson,
with sounds of whistles and ka-ching droning
down the hall. This can be a dying town
waiting to be rescued by outlet malls
and sweet cocktails. I can be sitting next
to a man fast on bets, casual with lies.
But I am here with you, brazen with love,
ready to walk me out to the sea where
Monet painted his sky blue and wavelets gray,
to breathe in greedily the harsh briny air.

YELLOW PLUM SEASON

*"Do you remember?" My sister asked
during a long distance phone call.*

My rainy city, no longer a colony,
it's heart not quite Chinese, but never British.

I went back in the rainy season,
moisture so thick you could part it with chopsticks
and clothes drooped on the clothesline like sedated patients.

Fog bloomed in the harbor.
Sounds of engines and long sirens,
ferries and sampans crisscrossed the chaotic water.

I went back to the back streets twisting
like weeds in the crevices, the best herbal shop
still brewing sweet soy, aroma that would calm even a thief.

Ink ran amok from soaked newspapers
as if it too had enough bad news.

The stationery shop, my small joy, filled with
calligraphy brushes. I smoothed my fingers along the tips,
over wolf hair, goat hair, rabbit hair.

And spent years learning to steady my wrist
for the stroke to flow like clear water.

"Memory is moistened with tears," said a local poet
and I could hear the blind musician playing an Erhu.
His long sad notes split open my heart
and I knew childhood lived there.

Days of Yellow Plum Season,
not quite spring or summer.
Days of sweaty floors and crying walls.

I went back as a child of divorce,
pleading allegiance to no one.

II.

新心
(New Heart)

我想在一個
愉快的遊行中消失
牽着一個
如在 Albert Lamarisea 電影裏
的紅汽球
從另一邊冒出
就像活在永恆裏
的孩子一樣
為它不休不眠

我想前往一座
陌生的城
在廣場上奏我的舊口琴
那兒的居民
曾經歷死亡多於出生
曾比護照辦事處
目睹更多的離別
但仍欣喜地
帶我去看
城裏最向陽的房子

夜裏當風
在我扰上咆哮
窗板像船難般打抖
我想謹記
一顆明亮的星
雖然它不會復返
它的餘光
足我能夠在那詛咒
的黑暗中行走

NEW HEART

I want to disappear into a happy parade,
come out the other side with a red balloon
like the one in Albert Lamorisse's movie
and lose sleep over it
as children do when they live
in a place of timelessness.

I want to play my old harmonica in the piazza
of a town whose language I don't speak
and whose inhabitants have witnessed
more death than birth,
more partings than the passport bureau,
yet jubilantly show me the sunniest house.

At night when the wind howls around my pillow
and the shutters shake like shipwrecks,
I want to remember one bright star
that is no more, but what light
it still left, enough for me
to walk through the damning dark.

DIPPING INTO THE BLACK POOL TO TOUCH THE FLOWERING ALMOND

Adrift for weeks
my heart returns
as a dream to its dreamer
the world hasn't changed
its sorrow is the same
but the morning on this day
does not oppress
the cat crouches
by the window
captivated by
a string of light
as if it's a live thing
I face the day
without a need to
rush forward or run away
a faint voice rising
from memory's black pool
I hear myself counting
as I climb a flight
of terrace stairs
to a no-name hill
of my forgotten city
which happens to be in
a season of bloom

FIRST MOVING DAY

I can't remember who put me
in the back of a rickety wagon
next to the rattan bookcase
and a chest of drawers,
to be pedaled to our new home—
"one with an elevator and a balcony,"
said my mother.
Her voice was her usual
at the breakfast table, betraying
not a hint of excitement or hurt.
We were leaving my grandparents' house,
its ancestor-blessed walls
and all the unfinished battles.

In the shades of the Banyan Trees,
a letter-reader read to the grannies,
the domestics haggled the price of eggs,
and I was being pulled toward a future
by a stranger, a tanned, mute man
whose two white sleeves puffed up
in the wind.
Soon the streets would be blurred
and I would be lost, over and over,
coming off the elevator, exiting
all the wrong floors.
Soon I would have myopia.
I would have to answer to life.

EGG WOMAN

That summer my mother was heartsick
and couldn't cook for us.

Around ten each morning a woman came
calling: fresh eggs, fresh eggs, fresh eggs.

I handed her a dollar for five
then held each one out to the sun.

Each day she was impatient: my eggs
are all good.

In the light each shell became
translucent:

I wasn't looking for decay,
I was looking for a cure.

MONSOON (1967)

When we get back the harbor is bloated again,
late night ferries bobbing on the water
like lanterns held by angry men. Fog this thick,
we will eat canned meat and pickled
mustard-greens for weeks, then pass around
the table bowls of rice gruel.
When the market opens, we wait in line
to buy flour and peanut oil, wait in line
to send the food packages off
to villages in Canton.
We wait obediently, then absent-mindedly.
By the time we come to the postal clerk's window,
none of us could remember our relatives' names, or
those whose hands are still tied behind their backs,
floating face down from the Pearl River, each
in his swollen goat-white skin: for
this is monsoon, mad rain hung
before us like a sheet of ghost.

YESTERDAY MORNING

My son came to my dream
because that was something
he could still do.
He sat on the edge of my bed,
not saying much until I drifted
to sleep, then he called out *mom*!
His voice was urgent and it startled me
and I knew he was there with me.
It was as if he has never died.

When I woke I told no one.
I made breakfast, ate it in the garden.
Then I thought the passage
back to this world was not impossible.
He was going to do it, to crossover
whenever he could.

EVEN IN DREAMS THERE ARE REASONS

There are no more tickets to where you want to go.
The clerk shakes his head, unsympathetic.

You open your wallet and find all the bills
are counterfeit, the dignified figure has been replaced
by a clown, laughing at you from the center.

Your bankcards are colorful and crisp, but fraudulent.
The clerk secretly dials the authorities,
soon a man flashes his badge near the exit.

You unfold a newspaper clipping and discover
the scandalous articles are about you, though
you can't recognize yourself in there.

A gang swarms from behind the kiosk and they want
your watch, your shoes, every bit of your life.
And they have the tickets.

When your son died, you said you don't want to live
anymore. In this dream, he is asleep in the other room.
He misses the train and is late for school.

You try to wake him with kisses. You have to get him
there so he can sit in front of his desk
and open a pile of books again.

Even if it means you have to face off the thieves, your accusers
and the ticket scalpers of this world.

SELF-PORTRAIT AS A FLUORESCENT LAMP

I am back against the ceiling,
my torso encased in a translucent shell
(made of plastic, cannot rot).

I have two long, parallel hearts,
each stretching to the opposite side
of my equator.

When jolted, I light up.
In the beginning, it was a dimmed light
always ahead of me.

Then came a white-heat light,
a slow but steady burning.
Lately, my light is a cool gray,

color of sky after harvest
when the field begins
to abandon itself.

I am happiest when left alone,
preferring shadow but attend to my duty,
I caress things:

the small porcelain cup bearing
scent of a summer fruit;
an outdated map naming the wrong countries;

the red mandarin coat that traveled
continents, a forest
of swaying bamboo freshly embroidered.

There are days when everything is
a grainy blur, when I flicker
like a blind moth.

What would I be without my shell?
Where to mark the scars,
where to store the chasms between my hearts?

Someday a hand will flick the switch,
I will go out
and leave the room black.

WHILE A FEVER BURNS TIME IS ELONGATED

Let there be light, words scribbled on the fridge,
and the dentist's number, a list of things
to buy. Something will explode. Something has.
Then *hope* is what I hear on Sundays, then
it's for a world I can't know. The choirs sing,
many mouths open wide into a void.
Somewhere, fields of lilies dying onto
themselves. We breathe, the one thing we still do.
A leaf twirls in a circular motion
refusing to come down. Progressively,
the room has grown large, empty as the sea.
It gives nothing back except breakage. On
the stove a low blue flame, outside in the
car-park, ice, slush, ice, slush, clouds racing clouds.

HOW TO LIVE IN A FUNK

(after Eleanor R. Taylor)

First, build yourself a trapdoor
let your cringed soul wander
like a dog with its tongue hanging out.

Remember: it's only a funk, only a state
of being like a daydream or inertia,
snap out of it when you are ready,
ready as the frozen smile forever saying *please*.

Keep pain in check. Practice don't-tell.
Blame it on the weather, how
heat drains you, rain empties
you. It's the sinus, never tears.

Feign hard and lie harder.
When asked, say you like it, yes, yes
yes and you want more. Say Thank You.

And when your island of sorrow
rises from beneath you, rise.
Float, feel
how it is, without gravity.

MEMENTOS

My grandmother's plastic soapbox; pink
Her voice, wash water on sunned cement
My friend's dictionary, her inscribed
    Chinese characters, straight and square
My son's sea-moss hair
My grandfather's poem about monkeys
    and his dream of following them
The ballerina figurine is what my mother sings
    to, after my father turns deaf

The snow-blinded alley waits for me
The boy on the snow, pushing
    himself up, is my son
The precarious journey is our journey
Every morning even the faintest stars check out
The stars are those you love, they are not
    God's stalking telescope
The ink stroke in my friend's calligraphy is her spine
My son and his gannets are flying away, are flying away

ASLEEP IN A FOREIGN CITY AFTER A LONG FLIGHT

I don't know where I am or what will be next.
I hear a fury of church bells, a heavy shuffling of wings.

I stir without waking. My mind placid
as taffeta, subjected to the will of winds. My dream

pushes away, orphaned. In a small hotel bed,
I sleep and sleep as though I've gone home from exile.

But even with my eyes closed I feel you are here.
For too long your absence stretches the hour

and occupies the cities I visit. I want
to tell you what happens on my way here,

how I have to trudge through a winter plain. Stars
the only direction. There are others like me numbed

to the marrow trying to cross thickets of snow.
The border guards shout at us as if we were refugees.

Some give up and slip into the ice. I keep going
because you are waiting. I imagine you up there

in a crow's nest, among tall trees and a wedge of moon,
peering anxiously into the binoculars. All the while

cities fly by, the roads zigzagged. I tell you
sometimes I want to stay, sometimes to go.

A HAT FOR THE SEA, TWO VOICES

(after Marie Etienne)

    You say you will buy a hat
    for we are going to the sea
    and the sun is fierce

    The sun is fierce   as is the wind
    which may blow your hat off
    send it up the bluff   crash it
    like a wounded kite   to retrieve it
    you have to pore over bodies
    wake them from their bronze dream

Wake them from their bronze dream
They are sunbathers like us
They know how it is to have a hat blown away
One of them will catch mine from midair
as if it's a boomerang boomeranging back
It makes them happy to think
some things are retrievable

    Some things are retrievable
    Or they may throw sand in our face
    Curse us in their language   language
    that sounds like waves   sighing
    and heaving   we don't know what's inside

We don't know what's inside
but remember how we love the sand
whiter than coconut flesh
We write on it over and over
and it bears us again and again
as if we have inlaid it with the most precious jewels
Dear—you can wear my hat to the burnt of the sun

        After I wear your hat   after it shields me
        from the burnt   I don't feel like losing it
        to the path of waves   their sighing and heaving
        as they wash up husks   of once living things
        as they rush out to   a quicker vanishing

IF

>*(after Kevin Young)*

The night folds up
like an origami crane, crisp on

both sides. The moon does
its own thing: that is, waning,

waning over so many roofs.
I wanted to howl at it

like my neighbor's unloved dog
until I exhausted my voice

on the world. Then,
as still as a

gecko, I
go to sleep.

TSUNAMI

The poet compares grief to carrying
a heavy box up the stairs.

I imagine myself with this box
upon an endless flight of stairs, well-worn,
stairs made of steel or stone, spiraling.

I keep climbing. My heart pounding,
lifting what I can't lift, no one is there to help.

Give me this. I would rather crush this box
into my chest, pushing what I can't push. Grief
is not like carrying a heavy box,
or being on a roller-coaster,
or riding a tsunami wave.

Grief is grief, like dead is dead.

AFTERWARD

Night, roofless, is pure black.
There is nothing on your eyelid,
no orange glow.
Count anyway. Name the unborn.
Number the spidery spine
of fish, reptiles, cradle the sea.
Let your dead go.
Let them come back with halos
flare like a just-fired pistol.

THE ELM TREE IN FRONT OF THE PHARMACY

Say to it what you will, the tree is three stories tall.
Its branches give shade to a few windows, its roots
push up the sidewalk. Two years now, red, white & blue
ribbons loop around it, then yellow. People leave photographs
of the old evening skyline, indigo blue still tugs like teen love.
At first, kids tagged poems on the trunk, drawings
of black smoke and angels went up too.
Then rain and snow washed them away.
We filled our days making pastas, baked loaf after loaf
of bread as if we didn't know what we hungered for.
Now all that's left are a few plastic orchid stems,
twining around a fresh ribbon someone just put up.
Of course we don't always notice these changes, these erasures
and remembrances, the way we don't notice
the crease between our eyebrows, the scab
that's grown thick around our heart. And when we do,
like coming home today, I found myself
looking at the tree and recognized at last,
an old friend, limping, is here to stay.

SONNET FOR AN ANT

I watch you crawl to my doorsill, a speck
of twig dragging behind like the cross, your
back droops. When you see me you stretch your neck.
What can I give now? Dear ant, this late hour.
Sorry I am not for either of us,
more incredulous, how you stagger out
some god-forsaken sinkhole, hungry plus
blind, shiver from stone to stone where nothing sprouts.
Like you to the waiting world I burrow
my way back and find the June mango sun
burnt to its wick, to live in this sorrow
I roll prayers on my tongue till there're none.
Go. Find your own honey trail, your droplet
of rain, your bread for the fable banquet.

REPAIR

The worker came with his sledgehammer, saw,
by noon the front stoop of my house crumbled
into fist-size mortar as if a war
had raged through. After he left I chiseled,
smoothed a corner of wall, snaked down exposed
pipes clogged with mold, taped up loose, useless wire.
Even sad, ruinous things should be disposed
properly, not left to burn like hellfire.
That night in my dream I beat at the door,
bolt shut, without which I could not get back
in, let myself walk the long corridor,
empty every room of its bric-a-brac,
see at the clearing a sun stained flower,
lodge it in my eyes if just for this hour.

SONNET FOR A NEW COUNTRY

for Tim

In front of the used bookstore I wait. Soon
the man I love will cross the avenue,
waving, perhaps humming a new blue tune.
Amidst a riot of lights he'll continue
to dart, like a dancer with two quick feet.
Spring is again here. Magnolias blaze
past the drab buildings, into the dim street
of memory where we turn back and gaze:
each bloom a pink dream radiantly lit.
Darling, who knows how the story goes, what
can we believe in the end? Bit by bit
the pages turn whether we get it or not.
But now night pulses hard, I learn to wait
once more. I see you: my answer to fate.

MY POET

He writes so hard
on the table
that it rattles
dictators and henchmen
from the dead
and their faces float up
in his head
like holograms,
along with the belly dancer,
headdress studded
with zircons, bluer
than the Star of Josephine,
swaying her full hips
in an immigrant bar lounge
on the outskirts of town
where men from a long voyage
have not forgotten
about seasickness
or the palm trees
weaving in and out
of their sleep like ghosts.

LOOKING OUT TO JAVA ROAD ON A CLOUDLESS DAY

All summer I smell the wild orchids in my native island.
Outside the streets have been dug up, leaving a film of dust
on our windows. We thought it was cataract.
Early geography lesson: above the courtyard, a square sky
letting in long days of sun or rain.
The island crouches in the sea like a bullfrog.
The locals called Hong Kong *cement fortress*,
a way to say nobody cared.
Last time I checked, a thirty story hotel has gone up on Java Road.
I want to stay there and then not.
Cities blend together outside time.
Memories and dreams have no rules.
Does the path to St Jude's Primary School still exist?
Has anyone else remembered there were fifty-eight steps?
After the killing, the courtyard was strewn with chicken feathers.
My grandmother wiped clean the knife to set the ancestral table.
The sutra we mimicked together must be incomprehensible
to her as it was to me. *How* does one turn around from
the Bitter Sea which has no end? That is the question.
An older girl in a beige summer dress, her long black hair flowing,
impressed upon me for the first time the idea of beauty.
Beauty in the midst of chaos, orchids left alone on the path.
"Down with the Paper Tigers!" "Down with the Imperial Dogs!"
The mob screamed, thrusting their red books into the air.
Up north, Red Guards roamed town to town smashing temple gods.
We smelled teargas throughout the summer,
dreaming of prom dresses.

Rumors had it that the English smuggled containers of cash out
and the ship stalled in South China Sea. The students chained
themselves to the fence, protesting a fare hike on Star Ferry.
Suddenly my sister brought copies of Nietzsche and Freud.
My father stopped coming home for dinner.
I started writing words by a small glow lamp.
Night swelled in thick heat.
My mother's father found his way to our front door
with just a wicker suitcase. In Hai-Kou, he surrendered
all his rental properties to the Communists so they let him go.
With us, he refused to use anything that's "Made in China,"
not even soy sauce. Don't ever tell him Mao is a great poet.
I wonder how many years had passed before he knew
he would never again see his hometown, or his wife
and their ten children, how it ate at him and made him
fidget all night staring at the unmoving stars.
I could have told him in this country they take your house too,
after they cart away your rocker, your television set,
your wife's flower pots on the porch.
I could have told him so much more and I am writing
this poem in a city whose name he had not heard of,
that I love the moon more than ever,
that home is the vessel which holds my words.
Yesterday I noticed a sun spot on the back of my hand, round
like a coin embossed with letters from a strange country.
I don't know how it got there.
Start again. Nothing budges.

THE BLUE JAYS

for MH, in memory

In the end
after the morphine
the nurse's visit

you search for
the names of birds
from your bone-white bed

III.

瞭望點
(Vantage Point)

夜裏飛機在上空飛過
翼燈像血石般拖曳

園裏有股腐朽果子的氣味
煤灰沈降在聖像上

夏天已差不多燃盡
我們從盤裏舉起酒杯

那令人陶醉的開始
已不和我們再扯上什麼

VANTAGE POINT

At night airplanes flew overhead,
their tail lights trailing like blood stones.

The air whiffed of rotten fruit,
soot had settled on the garden saints.

Summer was running itself out.
We lifted glasses from the tray

to the intoxicating beginnings
that had nothing more to do with us.

IF THE ANGELS ARE WATCHING

Mess everywhere. The drain's clogged.
The lock's jammed in this heat.
And the carpenter bees have eaten
a side of the shed, which threatens
to collapse, and will go down with
the sorry bird nest. On the news,

an elevator free falls twelve stories.
Bullets mistake a toddler for a doe.
And a man goes home with a new
knife, hidden in his duffel bag.
"State the location of this call…"
the operator in a monotone repeats,
knowing we can retract nothing.

Once more the rescue truck backs out
of the driveway into our street of wrecks.
Once more we watch in a daze till
a flock of geese appear, dark as pews,
their shrieking long and sharp,
something is always amiss.

BESLAN

> *(found poem)*

> *But even if I marry again ten times*
> *I'll never have a child like that.*
> —The father Vova Tumayev spoke of his
> daughter, Madina, after the massacre, as
> reported by the New York Times.

That's her, that's her,
that's her at the beach;
that's also her and
here she is, here she is,
here, here she is;
there she is
in the countryside,
there also, and that's
her, too."

> *"Oof, this is difficult,"* he said, but
> he kept turning the pages.

There she is in Rostov,
there she is, too; there
she is with her mother;
here she is, she was tall,
almost as tall as me;
that's her, too,
and that's her, too,
and that's her,
and that's also her,
also her, also her;
there she is with her friends,
that little girl died, too,
there she is
waving.

STRAWBERRIES

Her son dies in a car crash.
The friends with him that night all live.
The most injured one spends a month in rehab,
then returns to the university.
She, too, returns to her job in the local market,
packing fruit or working the cash register.
"It's in the little things." The coworkers speak
of the mother, noting how she stops
smiling and snaps at the customers.
But soon everyone adapts to her mood
the way they would adapt to seeing in the dark.

Summer comes to the valley.
There is so much green that the eyes hurt.
Wildflowers bleed on the roads,
shabby old barns re-emerge, sagging just a bit.
Then the out-of-towners arrive, looking
for antiques and the country store.
They come to the market sniffing this and that,
sampling honeys and thick jams.
Inevitably, one of them will bring a box of strawberries,
luscious, blessed, overflowing strawberries
to the cash register. Then another mother,
her voice filled with the thrills of summer,
cries, almost trilling,
"Aren't these the glorious?"

THE BELIEVER

On this side of the canal, iridescent green with anti-freeze,
you can walk blocks on end without seeing
anyone holding a tennis racket or a holy book.
The man at the car shop is banging away at a bent tire rim.
He works late into the night fixing parts and what he can't fix
he throws them out and far. He repeats this everyday, after coffee,
after clearing his head of nightmare and mirage. On Sundays,
he puts on a clean shirt and drives crosstown to the bowling alley.
Sometimes he thinks time is running out. The sun simmers
in the flimsy blue sky like a brass ball ready to strike.

DIFFICULT MUSIC

Across the lobby the daughter
waves to her mother who has come
to see her off, clutching a large shopping bag.
They sit together near the bulletin board
and watch the announcement of departing trains
and track assignments. The station is teeming
with travelers leaving after the holidays.
Snow has not begun though it is cloudy
and the wind has picked up since noon.

The daughter resumes talking on the cell phone.
The mother fumbles about her bag.
She takes out a couple of tangerines,
hands them to the daughter who shakes her head
and continues with the phone call.
The mother tries again, this time extracting
a bottle of soda from the bag, again
the daughter shakes her head.
They go on like this for sometime.
People watch them from the row behind,
unsure which side they are on,
on this pendulum of offering and refusal.

Once more the mother presses a loaf of bread
into the daughter's hand. The daughter gets up
abruptly and walks toward the gate.
With everyone in the hall watching,
the mother yells out her daughter's name,
and knocks the shopping bag to the floor.
The daughter turns and sees her mother
crying white-hot tears, and the loaf of bread
flying toward her like a missile. All the while
the speakers blare, repeating instructions
on boarding, preceding each announcement
with the same obligated music.

AT DINER RETRO

We don't smoke here now or worry if
the couple in the corner, silently picking
at their plates, still love each other.
The waitress, flashing a smile like Sally Field
in the *Flying Nun*, cheerfully takes our order
of milk and key lime pie. Jukeboxes are back,
playing songs from a languid summer
in which the days multiplied like mosquitoes,
the sky a hard grind blue. No one vanished and
the scariest thing was thunder from the far hills.

A RAP FOR PROPHET ISAIAH

have you not heard
have you not known
we're *Chanel* suited
Gucci armed
Cartier fingered
and we believe *Our Savior*
in a pair of *Prada* shoes

have you not heard
have you not known
we're *Spa* treated
our pores unclogged
our nails *French* tipped
we spend hours
we spend days
we believe in the power of
love of self

have you not heard
have you not known
we take tea in the garden
lovers behind the curtains
we don't get sweaty
we don't get gassy
we don't get scabby

have you not heard
have you not known
we get it
we get it
new/ old
we don't care
we don't discriminate
we buy/ we pay
we buy/ we pay/ we buy

we pay/ we pay

BETWEEN THE RAIDS

February wind whips Odessa out of Coney Island.
A few men huddle on the boardwalk, hands deep
in pockets, exchanging news of the latest raid.
The pizza man from Pakistan, ten years kneading
the dough, taken by midnight police dressed
in riot gears, apparently has used fake paper.
On the avenue, behind the dime store counter,
another man who kissed his new wife goodbye
in Karachi, hits the cash register keys
and the liquid numbers blossom into green.
He has a green card and is no criminal.
He has nothing to do with all these rackets.
He dreams of his bride's passage: silk
and incense, mint and liqueur.
Her hair would have to be oiled and plaited.
They would have a portrait taken,
would stroll on Brighton Beach, side by side
with the Nigerian cabby and the Chinese cook,
would go to the waterfront to see Manhattan,
its skyscrapers floating amidst clouds,
would catch barges round the Gowanus Bay
where once, workers unloaded great stones from Europe.
We repair these brownstones now, he thinks,
we spend days on the scaffold sandblasting their facades,
re-pointing the cement joints, our knees shaken maybe
but we don't write overwrought letters, sail
them back and forth the Atlantic. Our women
don't pack tablecloths, sleep covers, or measure
yards of wool to bring to the New World.

A WOMAN IN BROOKLYN SAYS EVERYDAY SHE WALKS TEN MILES WITHOUT A DESTINATION

Sometimes the last leaves trembling
on the sapling bring tears to my eyes,
other times I walk by unmoved.

All sorts of things bled
to the ground, snow, piss,
dark berries in July.

I glance at passersby, some avert
their eyes and have the face of a winter lake.

I eavesdrop on Catholic schoolgirls
huddling at the feet of Mary Star of the Sea,
the statue with sealed lips.

I envy those who walk with jaunty steps,
switching off the world's clamor
with expensive earphones.

Along the way I argue with myself,
win by logic, rigid as a city grid.
Then I am back to where I began.

I walk as if the angry angels hover over me.

I walk circuitously, toward abandoned streets
toward another green light.

A forked road is the least of the problem.
I walk to walk out of myself.

I walk the way Scheherazade must keep telling the story.

I walk to keep myself from shrieking.

UNDER THE EXPRESSWAY

Sometimes at night, from our apartment windows, we catch
a cruise ship leaving the port, plowing headstrong into the dark.
We hear about the celebrity balls and lobster tails on ice.
We are not bitter. We go to bed as usual, at ease
with the sounds of metal gates grating the pavement,
car doors opening and slamming in front of the old porn shop.
Soon our neighbors come home from the night shift and briefly
have the city to themselves. They are not the kind to tell
how bad they have it. They look at you with a smirk or a longing,
smiles on their faces dim as a waning street lamp.

SWEET AND BITTER

My girl comes home smelling like chocolate.
All day she works in a candy factory, pouring hot
cocoa mix into the tin molds, turning out Santas
for Christmas, bunnies for Easter.
In the evening she takes long showers while I read Neruda
in bed, thinking about what he said on impure poetry:
"As a body, with its food stains and its shame."

"You smell like a chocolate haven." I say, sniffing
behind her ears and under her armpits like a puppy.
Sometimes she kisses me. Sometimes she slaps me hard.

When all is quiet and we nestle in the half sleep dark,
she says "I guess better than smelling like chicken grease,
or booze, or sex, or fear."

Oh baby, better than nothing at all.

TURTLE SOUP SONG

Vats of steam, smelly, downright
stinky. A man stops by, drinks
one bowl. Aphrodisiac.
Loosens his tie and goes on home.

The wife sips tea. Almond or
chrysanthemum. Eyes glued to
TV, playing *Burton* and
Taylor, in *Taming of the Shrew*.

HUDSON IN JULY

At last the sun wanes over the Hudson,
its honey lights slick the water, velvet
as a daydream with its boat and oarsman
who keeps rowing toward a new exit.
If this were the Ganges, girls in long, scented braids
would be wringing clothes in the rancid air,
barely turning to glance at the men, staid,
eyes drained of stars as they ready a pyre.

Here on the wharf, a brigade of children
congregate before the lit movie screen,
grow quiet as blades of light fall, then darken,
hollowing our faces where brightness has been.
Below us, pilings extend in water
like kneeling pilgrims, stranded in stilted prayer.

FATE

I don't know where the grandmothers are going
arm in arm as they complain, whispering like rain
falling, sometimes pausing to look at the boys
climbing up the monkey bars without shoes or fear
and Boo the bus driver eats his duck and rice
before heading out on the interstate to Atlantic City
where his paranoid brother used to drive and curse
at cars, trucks, even an army tank inching along
as in a funeral procession. Wet maple leaves slapped
on the windshield like fish skeletons and Boo's brother
screamed "Satan City!' as he crossed the Pulaski Skyway.
We looked at him like he was crazy and ate
our cream coconut buns and drank our coffee
with shots of whiskey till the Lady Clairvoyant
appeared in her real fur collar, her face a slice of moon,
insisting on telling our future for five dollars.

THE READER SPEAKS TO THE POET

Don't ask me to die for you.
No one I know is not moving toward her end.
A shortcut is not called for.

Don't say you will die for me.
I am tired of stunts, trapezes and clever bells.
I cringe at the exotic six-foot mollusk that
made you wet, the vertebrae of a dinosaur
so intricate you name all their parts.

Or please do not spread before me an ancient dawn,
a land of lollipops only you can lick.
You tour the victim museums and toxic dumps.
You come back with a polished indignation
and glow at the podium.

Don't say you will go inside language to find life.
Life is right here in this dust-fed room.
Say how you get out of bed each morning
when a funnel of light scans
and finds you empty.

Tell me what made you get dressed
then turn away from that sad figure
in front of the burnished mirror.

IN PRAISE OF A RAINY DAY

A rainy day, ordinary
but inevitable, it's autumn
again. Yes, we've been here
before. Easy as your breathing—
weather. You live in it.
It's the first thing you notice
when you get up in the morning,
deciding if you will open the door
and walk to the newsstand,
to the grocery store,
without fanfare,
bringing back today's supper,
something simple like rice
and beans, the day-to-day
sustenance that allows
you to live yet another day,
without having to strain
your neck to see
if the clouds are turning
into rose petals, or
a marching army troop,
that you are not so desperate
to be extraordinary
that you start meditating
on paper clips and thumb tacks
scattering across your desk
until you will them to life
as if that's the one thing
your lubricated mind wants
on an ordinary
but inevitable, rainy day.

AT CRATE & BARREL

We trek deeper and deeper inside the store,
reaching for the faraway world.

Here's the salad bowl,
made of Indonesian mango wood,
stained with the tropical moon.

There's a set of placemats,
made of sea grasses from the Philippine coast,
woven by women who live in thatched houses.

Glass wares that satisfy every desire,
the elegant platter, candy dish and gravy bowl, hand blown
by artisans with strong lungs and nimble fingers.

Polish crystals, Finnish textiles, the world beckons.
Can't we love them all?

These days it takes more and more
to feed our hungry house.

MAY AND LILACS

A scaffold above the new condo sways slightly.
The workers have arrived, waiting they gaze
at morning's brightness, for a moment
even the back alley gleams,
the sun not yet brutal.

People are in love with the city again.
Bikers in colorful jerseys loop around the park
bursting in pistachio green, tourists wave
giddily under the billboards while headlines spin.

We speak as if nothing can hurt us,
that the poor too have spring. Come love us,
feed us drunken blossoms.

We admit fear only to ourselves.
If the rope splits, if the plank snaps,
if one of the workers is suddenly blinded by the sunlight
volleying off the car roofs.

We have emerged from a long winter,
memory of black ice clings to our retina,
stinging us to tears at the sight of the sun.

LETTER TO K

I'm not responsible for all my thoughts.
I will not explain even if I could.
Be careful how you break a large glass bowl.
Rain is rain is no more than goddamned rain.
It takes courage to return the bouquet.
No one is happy when the light goes out.
When there's nothing left to do you can bawl.
The man on the horse vanishes in the trees.
Queens everywhere cling to their tiaras.
Heaven's a gossamer haze. Hell is hell.
To each other we say this is enough.
Have I told you I love you I love you.

INEXHAUSTIBLE DAYS

The cats yowl at a new day,
we get the news, read our horoscopes,
examine the merit of grass-fed beef,

Snuggie Blanket is all the rage
this Christmas, no child should live without
battery-charged hamsters,

another celebrity is caught cheating on his wife,
a million dollars in hush money.

The plumber overcharges.
The Hard Drive dies.

Our married friends are falling out of love.

Let's wait for a sunnier day,
the sofa can use new upholstery,

what's playing at the Cineplex?

We sail past tragedies and the dark-age,
artificial sun shines our windowless room,
our voice commands its temperature.

What other days do we have but inexhaustible days?

We make the same mistakes, apply the same metaphors,
sunset for eternity, sex for love, similes stretch out
like a line of limousines, the narratives

of what he did to me and what I did
to him, our poems are houses with no bones. Your art,

does it allow you to live more, for even just an afternoon

in the indifferent goings-on,
on days when no poem should come,
bastard days of the merely existed—
Search for poetry.

THE MOON FROM MY WRITING TABLE

Above the apartment buildings
where windows hold tense sleep,
and maps are useless.

At the empty stadium
where triumph and defeat
once shared the same bright light.

On a long country road
flanked by wheatfields and night crows,
conversation with god is resumed.

On faces of the gargoyles,
heeding warnings with their long tongue
and bulging eyes, terror I'm ignorant of.

Reflected in the idyll river,
always flowing backward
where someone I love is waving.

On the pages of my notebook,
tenuous as words, hoping
to be written into tenacity.

NOTES FROM MY FLIGHT BOOK

1.   *Where are you from?*

They ask
in foreign cities.
They ask
in your adopted country.
They ask
in your birthplace.
You ask yourself
in the restaurants' plate glass.

2.   The Midday Park in Montmartre

No grand greenway,
rare plants with exotic names,
just a quiet swing set, a bird bath,
the gaze of a poet under the chestnut,
pledging silence.

3.   On the Avenue of Temples

A warm wind sweeps the gold lighted streets,
trees bow like courtesans.
But there's no answer
when the mourners come for news.

4.   With Doubts

Some poets think it is desirable to write
from the fullness of mind, a state of awareness
which includes all thoughts & feelings.

Do they also mean madness, dark things
that flutter in *mind's* peripheral vision?
Let me write from the frost-bright heart
of the poem, like the moonshine
above Li Po's bed.

5.   Easy Target

If you hate the moon so much,
try outrunning it.

6.   Chinese New Year

My people like to chase away evil spirits
with firecrackers and gongs.
Every year red confetti rains over us,
size of a tear,
sticks to our faces, like hope.

7.   Sun & *Night*

The sun slips into the horizon
for the infinite time.
Still, you have to see for yourself
and decide— before *Night's*
extravagant arrival.

8.   River Cher

Gray and serious,
the river flows as if it is still grieving
with the inconsolable widow,
Louise the White Queen
in the Sixteenth Century.

9.   At Chateau de Chenonceau

In the huge kitchen quarters
there are coppery wares and harvest spreads,
mock aprons once worn by ladies-in-waiting.

I lift an apple from a large platter
laden with the lives of others, then a voice
drifts in,
if you could live the life of another, would you?

10.   *Time*

The persistent oarsman,
like the single-minded Olympian,
keeps rowing us away.

About the Author

Pui Ying Wong was born and raised in Hong Kong. She is bilingual in English and Chinese. She left Hong Kong to study in Japan before coming to the United States. She is the author of two chapbooks: *Mementos* (Finishing Line Press, 2007), *Sonnet for a New Country* (Pudding House Press, 2008). Her poems have appeared in both English and Chinese language journals. She lives in Brooklyn with her husband, the poet Tim Suermondt.

About NYQ Books™

NYQ Books™ was established in 2009 as an imprint of The New York Quarterly Foundation, Inc. Its mission is to augment the New York Quarterly poetry magazine by providing an additional venue for poets already published in the magazine. A lifelong dream of NYQ's founding editor, William Packard, NYQ Books™ has been made possible by both growing foundation support and new technology that was not available during William Packard's lifetime. We are proud to present these books to you and hope that you will continue to support The New York Quarterly Foundation, Inc. and our poets and that you will enjoy these other titles from NYQ Books™:

Joanna Crispi	Soldier in the Grass
Tim Suermondt	Just Beautiful
Ted Jonathan	Bones and Jokes
Fred Yannantuono	A Boilermaker for the Lady
Sanford Fraser	Tourist
Grace Zabriskie	Poems

Please visit our website for these and other titles:

www.nyqbooks.org

www.ingramcontent.com/pod-product-compliance
Lightning Source LLC
LaVergne TN
LVHW011428080426
835512LV00005B/332

9 781935 520290